GREENLAND

CANADA

NORTH AMERICA

UNITED STATES OF AMERICA

MEXICO

ATLANTIC OCEAN

PACIFIC OCEAN

VENEZUELA
COLOMBIA
PERU
BRAZIL
BOLIVIA
ARGENTINA

SOUTH AMERICA

ARCTIC OCEAN

EUROPE
ASIA
AFRICA
PACIFIC OCEAN
INDIAN OCEAN
ATLANTIC OCEAN
AUSTRALIA

SWEDEN
FINLAND
GERMANY
POLAND
UKRAINE
SPAIN
FRANCE
RUSSIA
KAZAKHSTAN
MONGOLIA
UZBEKISTAN
TURKMENISTAN
TURKEY
IRAQ
IRAN
AFGHANISTAN
PAKISTAN
CHINA
INDIA
MAURITANIA
ALGERIA
LIBYA
EGYPT
SAUDI ARABIA
MALI
NIGER
CHAD
SUDAN
YEMEN
OMAN
NIGERIA
C.A.R.
SOUTH SUDAN
ETHIOPIA
D.R. OF THE CONGO
KENYA
TANZANIA
ANGOLA
ZAMBIA
MADAGASCAR
NAMIBIA
BOTSWANA
SOUTH AFRICA
AUSTRALIA

Thank you for supporting the children in your lives by reading to them.

To my son: Never stop reading or dreaming.

To Dr. F. Friesen: Thank you for your advice. "Three books a day" has changed my life.

— Raina Schnider

To my family: Thank you for all the support in everything I do. It means the world.

— Alex Terakita

FriesenPress

Suite 300 - 990 Fort St
Victoria, BC, V8V 3K2
Canada

www.friesenpress.com

Copyright © 2018 by Raina Schnider
First Edition — 2018

Illustrator: Alex Terakita
Editor: Rachel Small

All rights reserved.

No part of this publication may be reproduced in any form, or by any means, electronic or mechanical, including photocopying, recording, or any information browsing, storage, or retrieval system, without permission in writing from FriesenPress.

ISBN
978-1-7751-3230-1 (Hardcover)
978-1-5255-2140-9 (Paperback)
978-1-5255-2141-6 (eBook)

1. FAMILY & RELATIONSHIPS

Distributed to the trade by The Ingram Book Company

MY CANADIAN FAMILY

Words by
RAINA SCHNIDER

Drawings by
ALEX TERAKITA

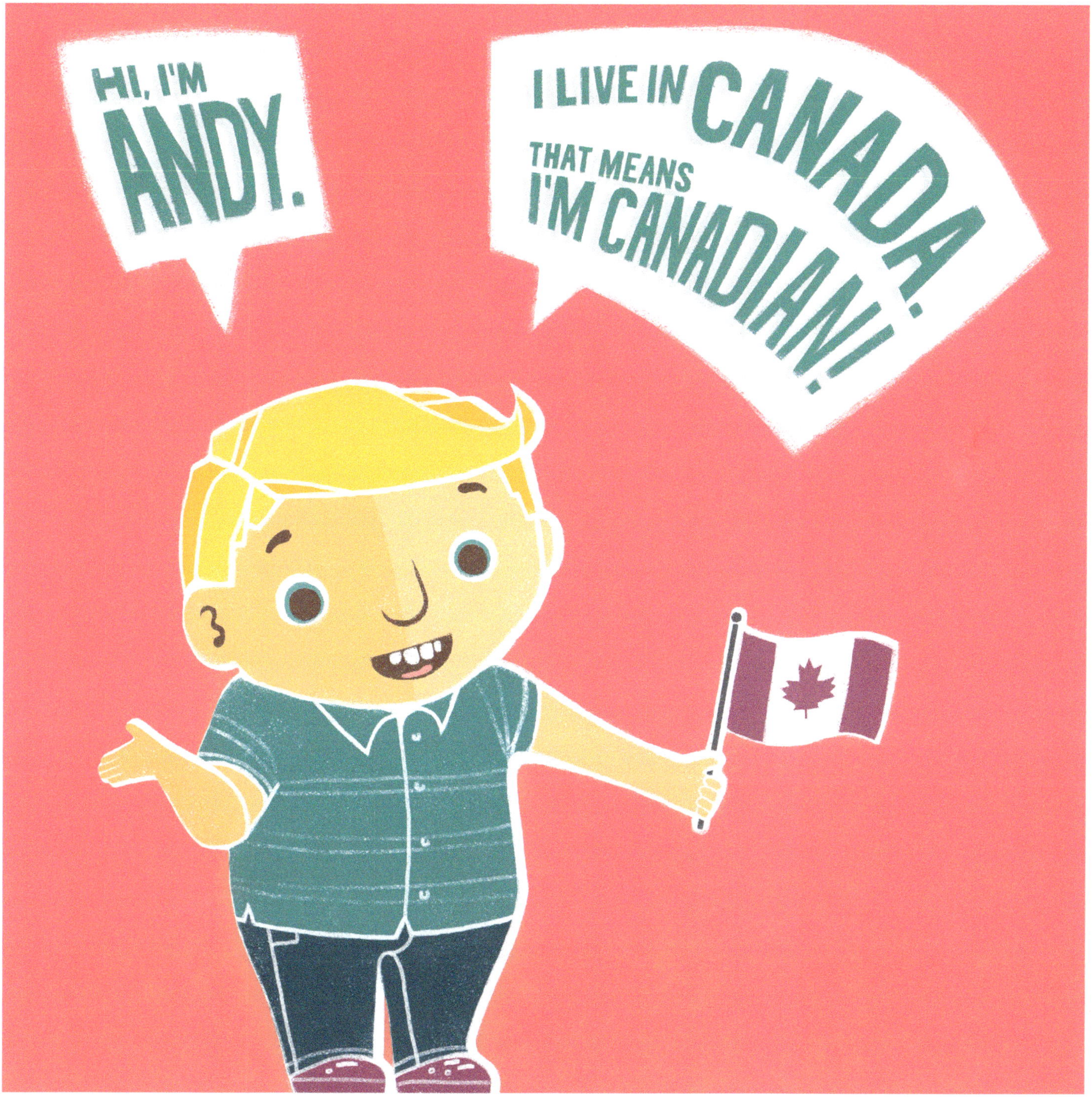
HI, I'M ANDY.
I LIVE IN CANADA.
THAT MEANS I'M CANADIAN!

Canadian families are all different. We speak different languages and have special traditions. Some *Canadians* even live outside of *Canada*.

Our differences are what make being *Canadian* so great!

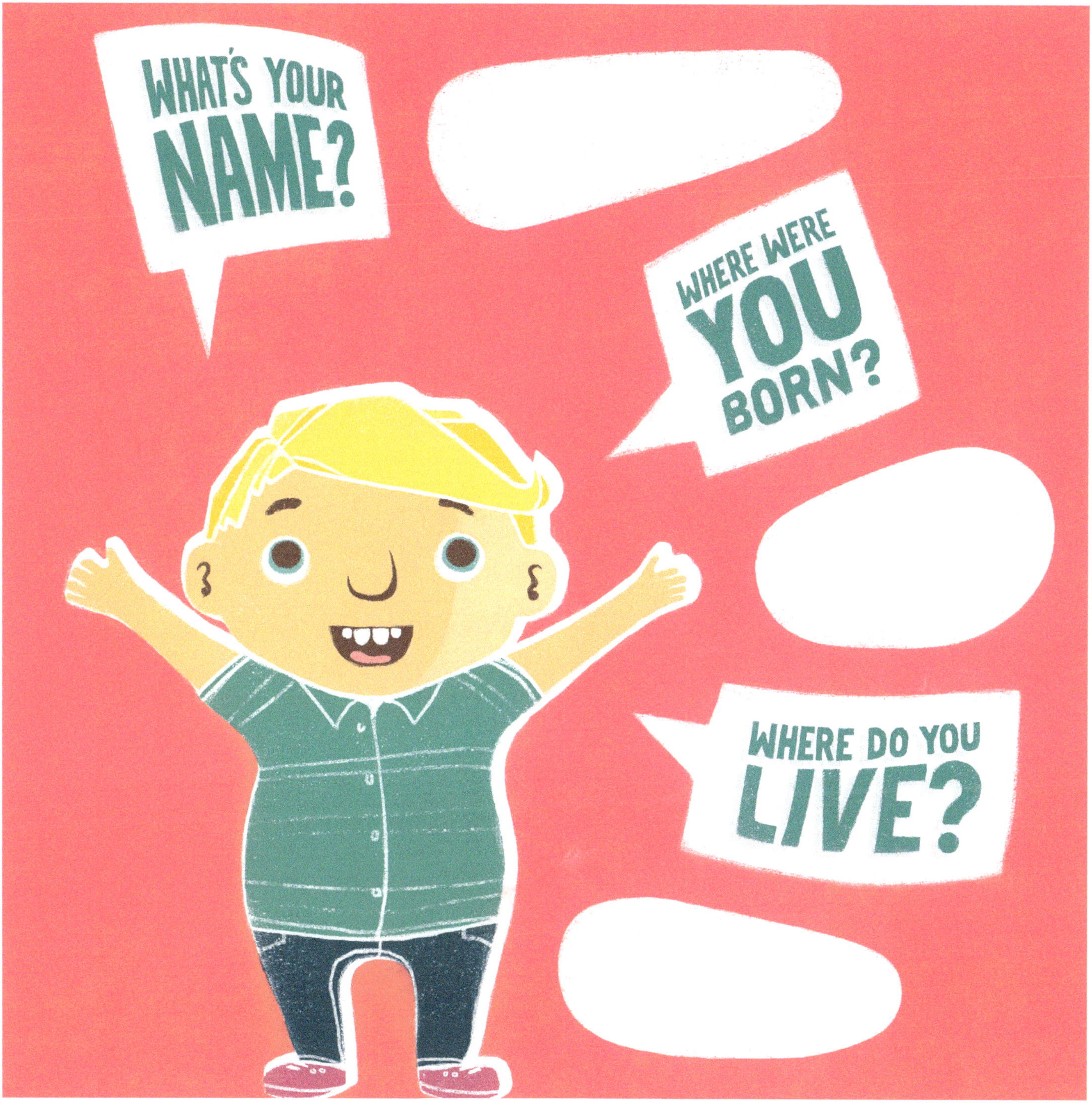
WHAT'S YOUR NAME?
WHERE WERE YOU BORN?
WHERE DO YOU LIVE?

I want to show you what my **Canadian** family is like.

My father was born in **Spain**, so he speaks **Spanish**. I call him *papá*. I have two last names, just like him. I call my mother *mamá*. She was born in **Canada**, but she speaks **Spanish**, too.

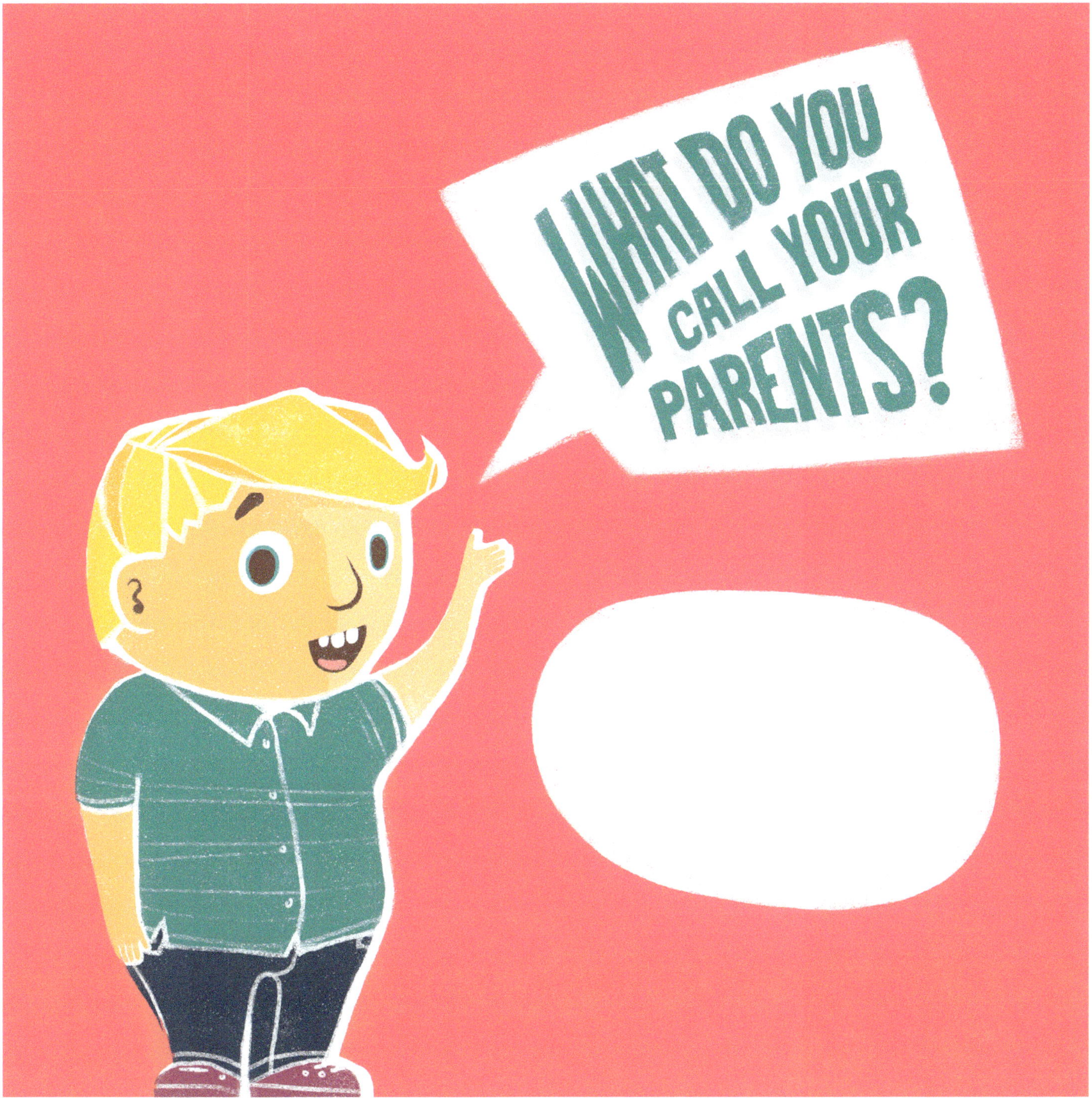
WHAT DO YOU CALL YOUR PARENTS?

My *mamá's* parents
are my *nana* and *opa*.

Opa was born in *Switzerland*.
He speaks *Swiss German*.

Nana was born in **Canada**. Her parents were from **Scotland** and **England**.

My *papá's* parents live in *Spain*.
I video-call them every week.
They are my *abuelo* and *abuela*,
and I speak *Spanish* with them.

What do you call your grandparents?

Dylan, Lainey, and Olivia have the same *nana* and *opa* as I do.

That means they are my **cousins**.

I have **cousins** in **Spain** and **Switzerland**, too!
I see Natalia, Asier, and Jennifer when we go
on vacation in the summer.

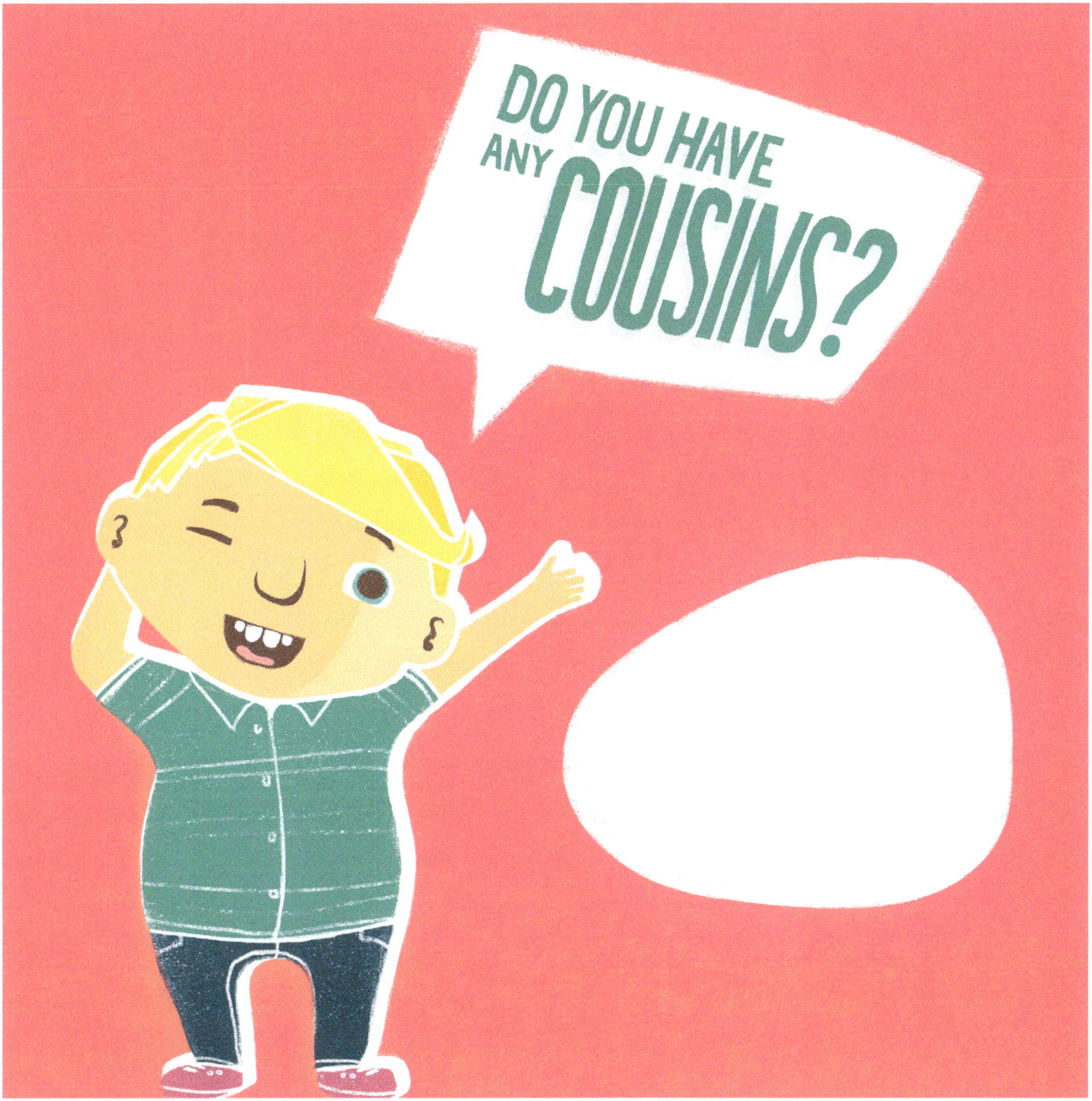
DO YOU HAVE ANY COUSINS?

Olivia has a *mom* and a *dad*,
but they don't live together anymore.

Olivia lives with her **mom,** and sees her **dad** on the weekend.

Families are all about *love*,
no matter what your gender.

My *cousins* Hugo, Eloise,
and Oliver have two *daddies*,
and they all live in *Australia*.

DO YOU HAVE MORE THAN ONE MOM OR DAD?
DO YOU HAVE MORE THAN ONE HOME?

We have a family reunion every year. Our **cousin** Eric and his family are part of the **Dene First Nations** people.

They include us in their family traditions by singing, playing drums, and celebrating their **ancestors.**

My family members come from all over to have a big party, even my **Canadian cousins** who live in **Panama**!

Jennifer speaks **Swiss German**.

Olivia, Lainey, and Dylan speak **English**.

Natalia and Asier speak **Spanish**.

Eric speaks **Dene**.

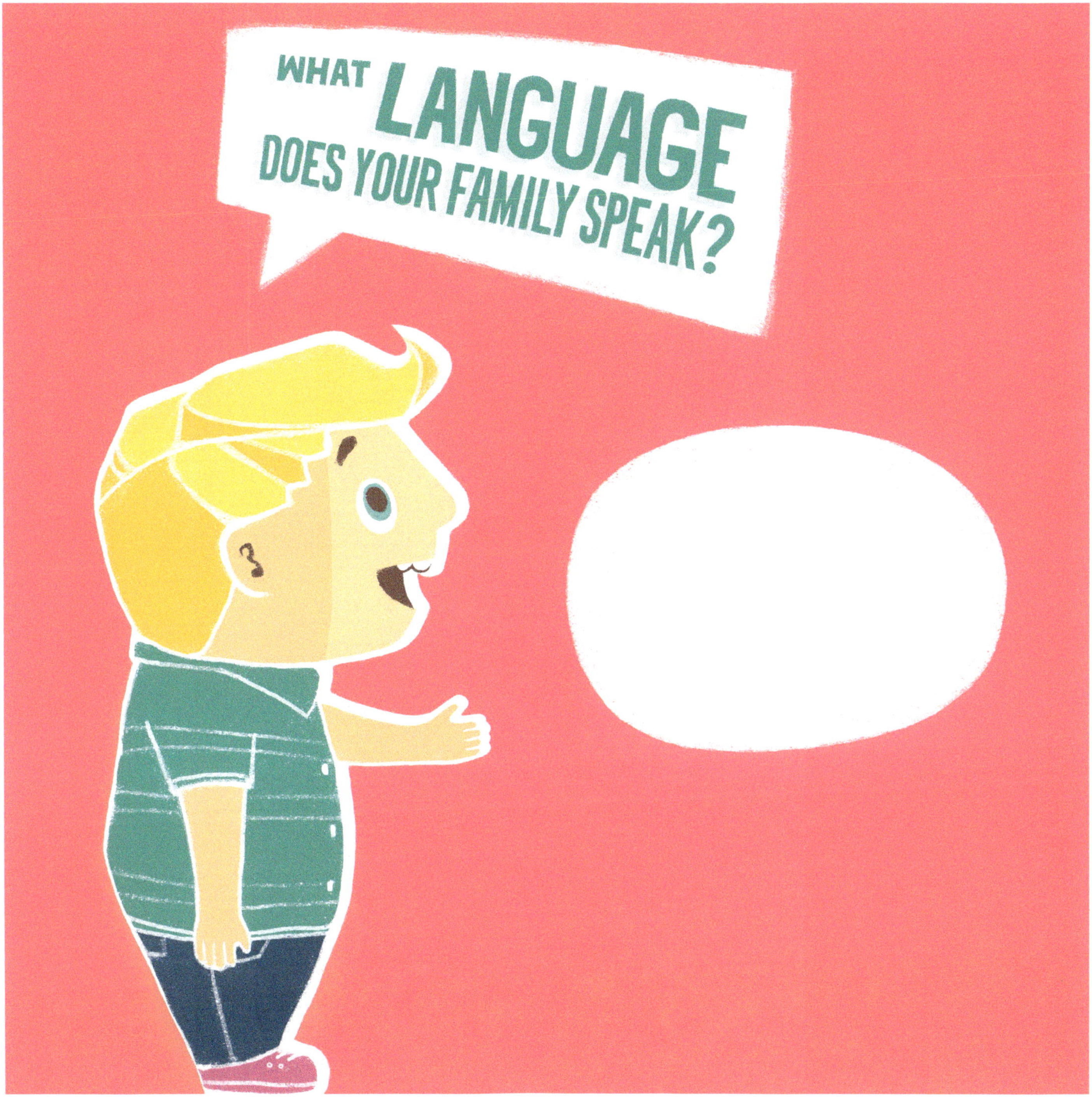
WHAT LANGUAGE DOES YOUR FAMILY SPEAK?

We have lots of friends who are part of our family, too!
My friend Wynter calls her mother *maman*
and her grandma *mémé*.

Wynter goes to see her *mémé* every day, and they practise *French* together.

This is my friend William.

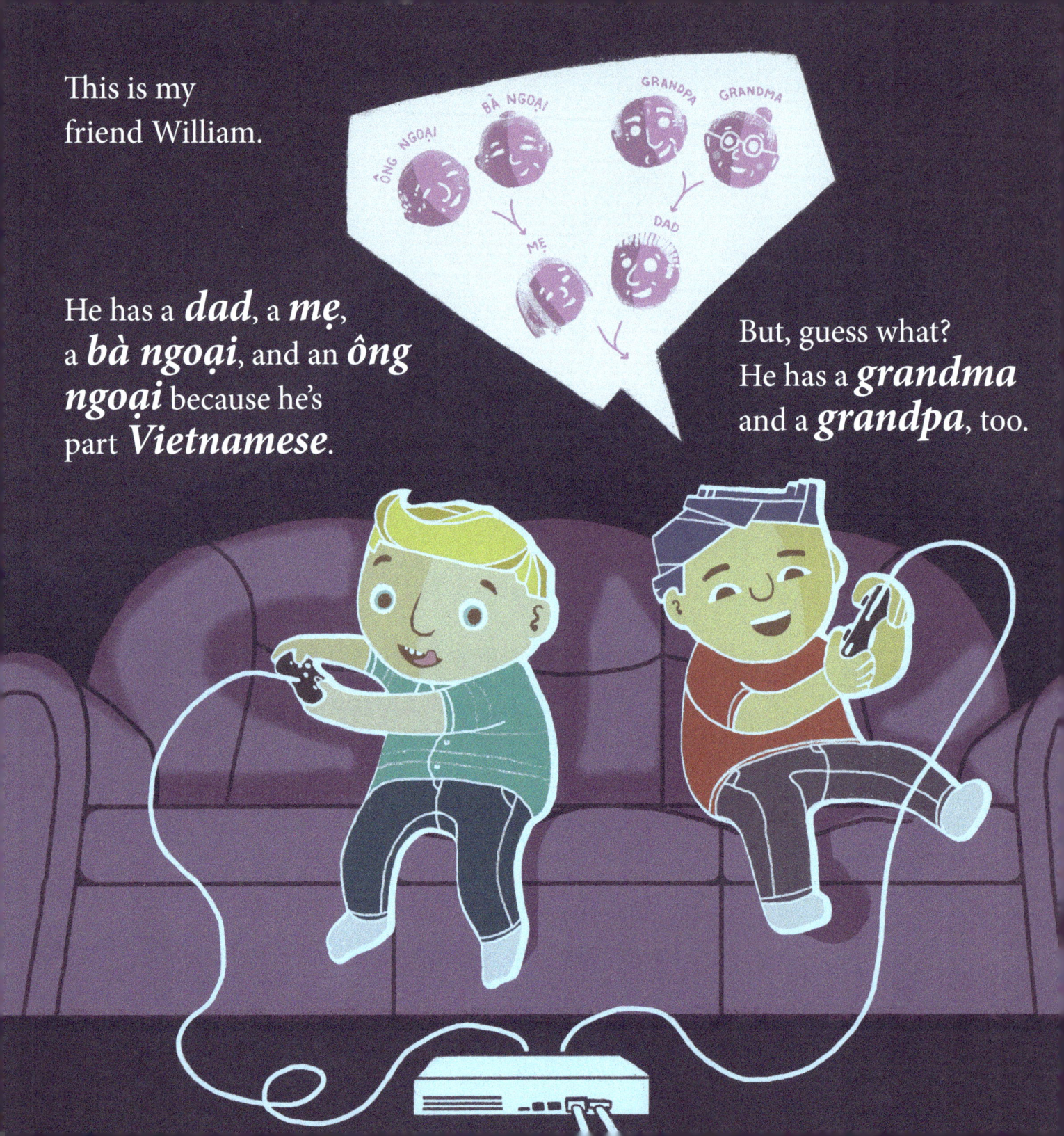

He has a **dad**, a **mẹ**, a **bà ngoại**, and an **ông ngoại** because he's part **Vietnamese**.

But, guess what? He has a **grandma** and a **grandpa**, too.

WHO ARE THE SPECIAL PEOPLE IN YOUR LIFE?
WHAT ARE THEIR FAMILIES LIKE?

Now that you know all about *me*,
I want to hear more about *you*!

What's your *Canadian* family like?

GREENLAND
CANADA
NORTH AMERICA
UNITED STATES OF AMERICA
ATLANTIC OCEAN
MEXICO
VENEZUELA
COLOMBIA
PACIFIC OCEAN
BRAZIL
PERU
BOLIVIA
SOUTH AMERICA
ARGENTINA

ARCTIC OCEAN
EUROPE
RUSSIA
SWEDEN
FINLAND
ASIA
GERMANY
POLAND
UKRAINE
KAZAKHSTAN
MONGOLIA
FRANCE
SPAIN
UZBEKISTAN
TURKMENISTAN
TURKEY
CHINA
IRAN
IRAQ
AFGHANISTAN
PAKISTAN
PACIFIC OCEAN
ALGERIA
LIBYA
EGYPT
SAUDI ARABIA
INDIA
OMAN
YEMEN
MAURITANIA
MALI
NIGER
CHAD
SUDAN
NIGERIA
ETHIOPIA
SOUTH SUDAN
C.A.R.
AFRICA
KENYA
D.R. OF THE CONGO
TANZANIA
INDIAN OCEAN
ANGOLA
ZAMBIA
MADAGASCAR
NAMIBIA
BOTSWANA
SOUTH AFRICA
ATLANTIC OCEAN
AUSTRALIA
AUSTRALIA

CPSIA information can be obtained
at www.ICGtesting.com
Printed in the USA
LVHW07s0809240418
574462LV00002BA/2/P

9 781525 521409